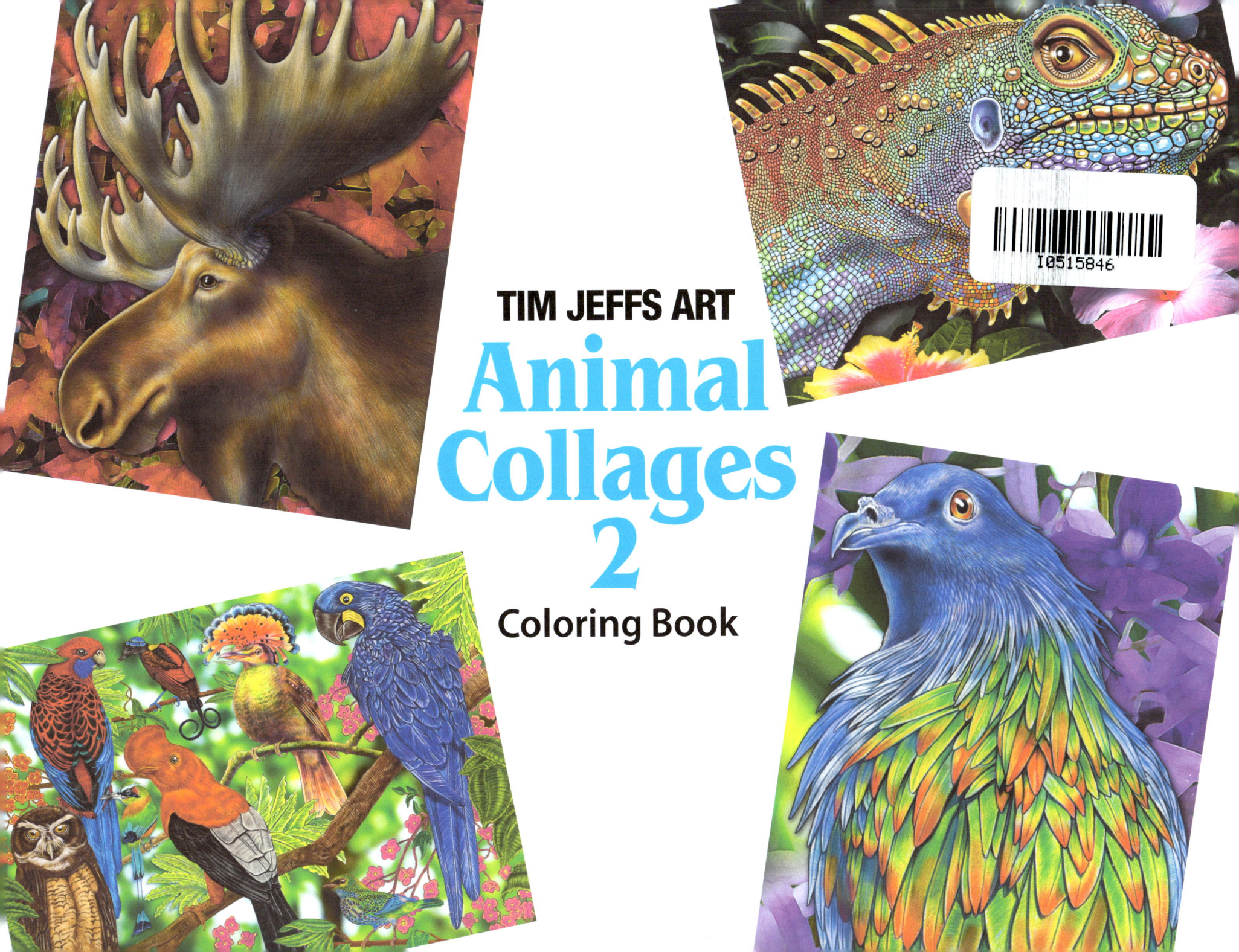

TIM JEFFS ART
Animal Collages 2
Coloring Book

Pictures That Tell A Story

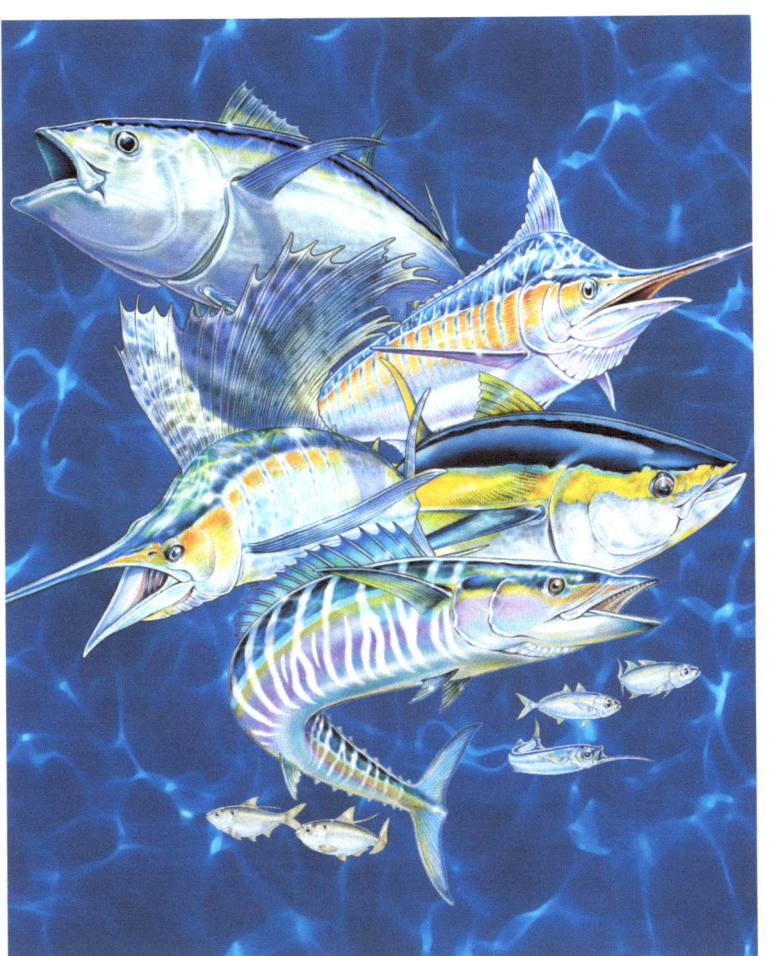

Themed Collages. Creating pictures that have similar animals within them can produce a picture that tells a story. I love doing this by bringing together all of my fish, birds, reptiles, etc into one image. A school of fish, a flock of birds, or a pod of whales. These groups of animals come to life in a collage. With the overwhelmingly kind response to my first animal collage coloring book I'm back with another! This second book in the series consists of 20 new animal collages I created from images I had drawn previously. I hope you will enjoy coloring these new collages as much as I had building them.

Tim Jeffs
Wildlife Artist

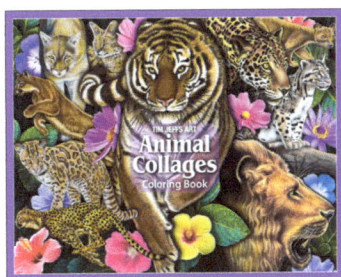

Also available
Animal Collages Volume 1

For Jane, Jenna and Harrison
Dedicated to all of the wonderful colorists who have supported my art and made my drawings more beautiful with their colors, and all the precious creatures that we live among.
A special thank you to Jo Warren and Karl Jennings for all of their continued support.

© Copyright 2023 Tim Jeffs Art

All rights reserved. No part of this publication may be reproduced or distributed in any form without the prior written permission of Tim Jeffs Art.

Tim Jeffs Art

376 East Madison Avenue, Dumont, NJ 07628

Animal Collages Index

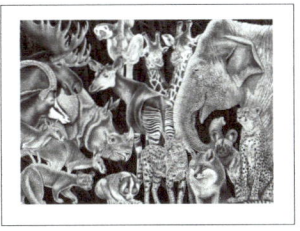
Animals of the World 1

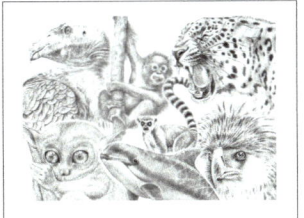
Endangered Species 5

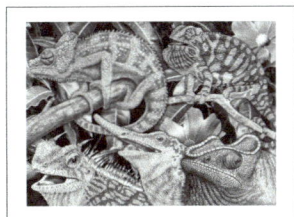
Lizards 9

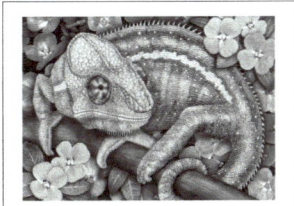
Panther Chameleon 13

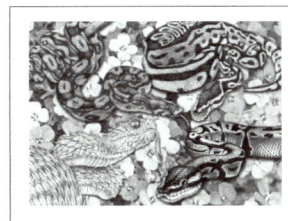
Snakes 17

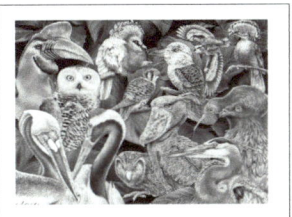
Birds of the World 2

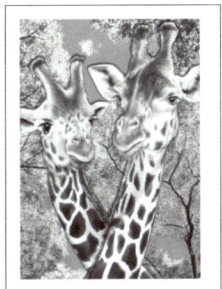
Giraffes 6

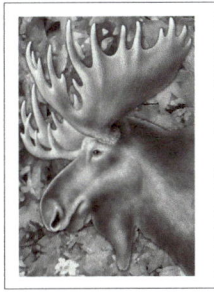
Moose 10

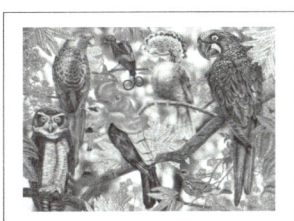
Rainforest Birds 14

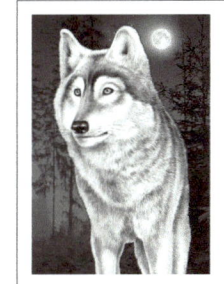
Timber Wolf 18

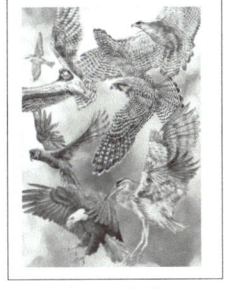
Birds in Flight 3

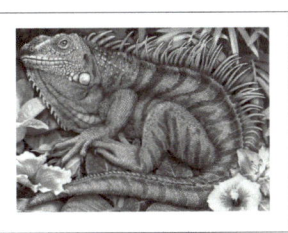
Iguana One 7

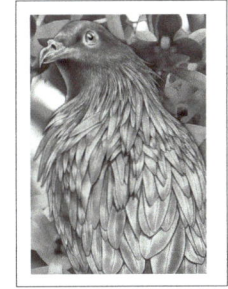
Nicobar Pigeon 11

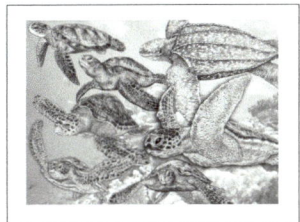
Sea Turtles 15

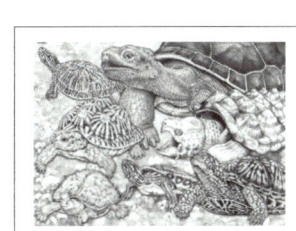
Turtles 19

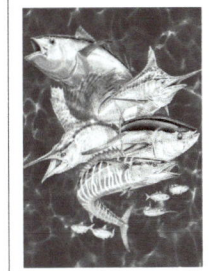
Deep Sea Fish 4

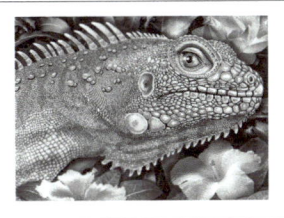
Iguana Two 8

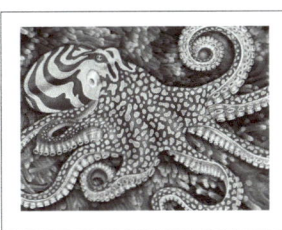
Octopus 12

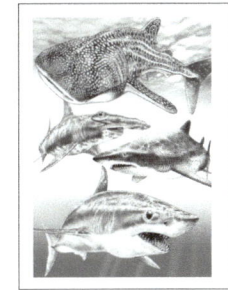
Sharks 16

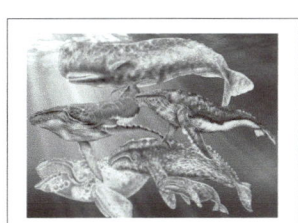
Whales 20

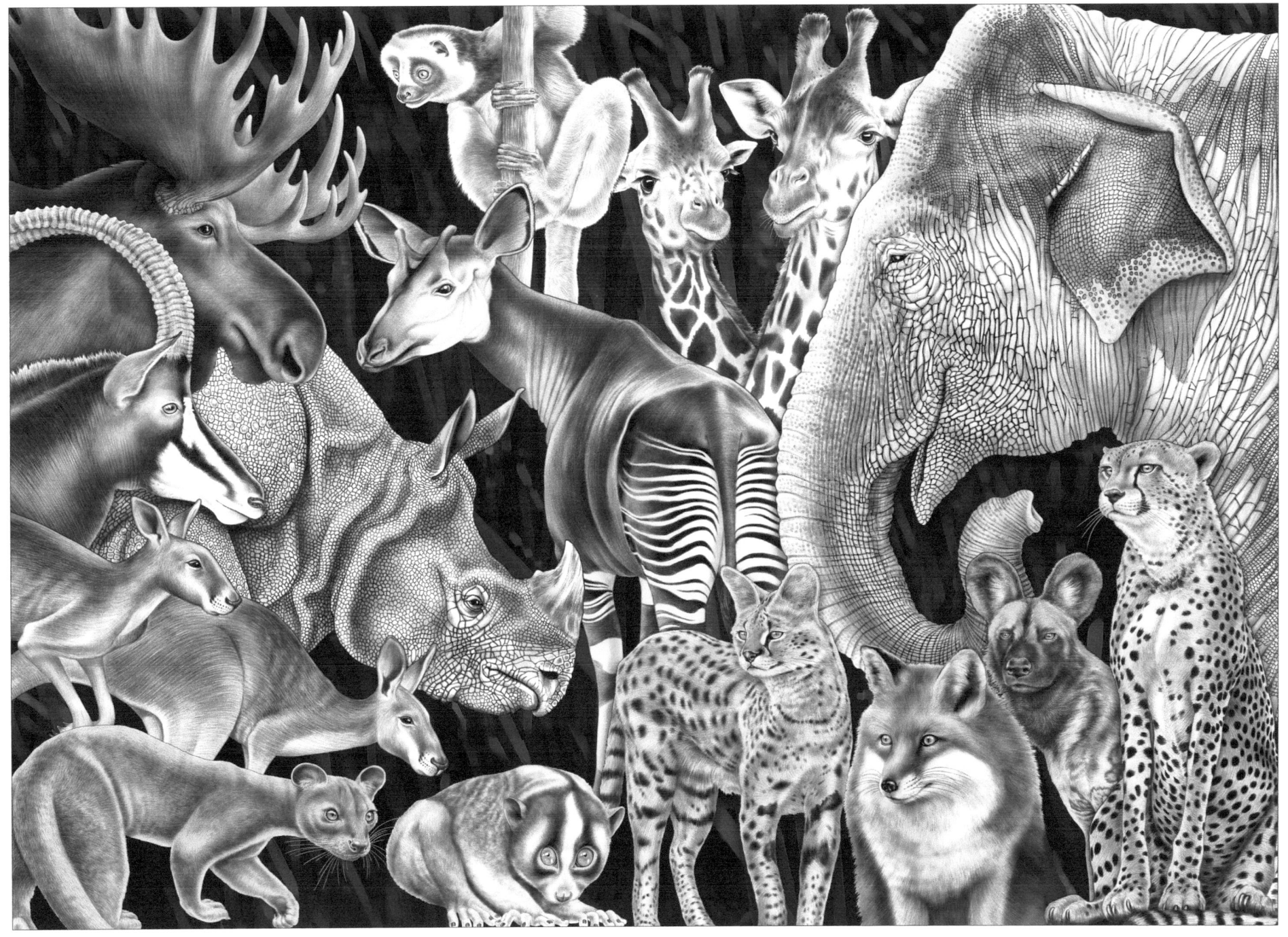

Animals of the World

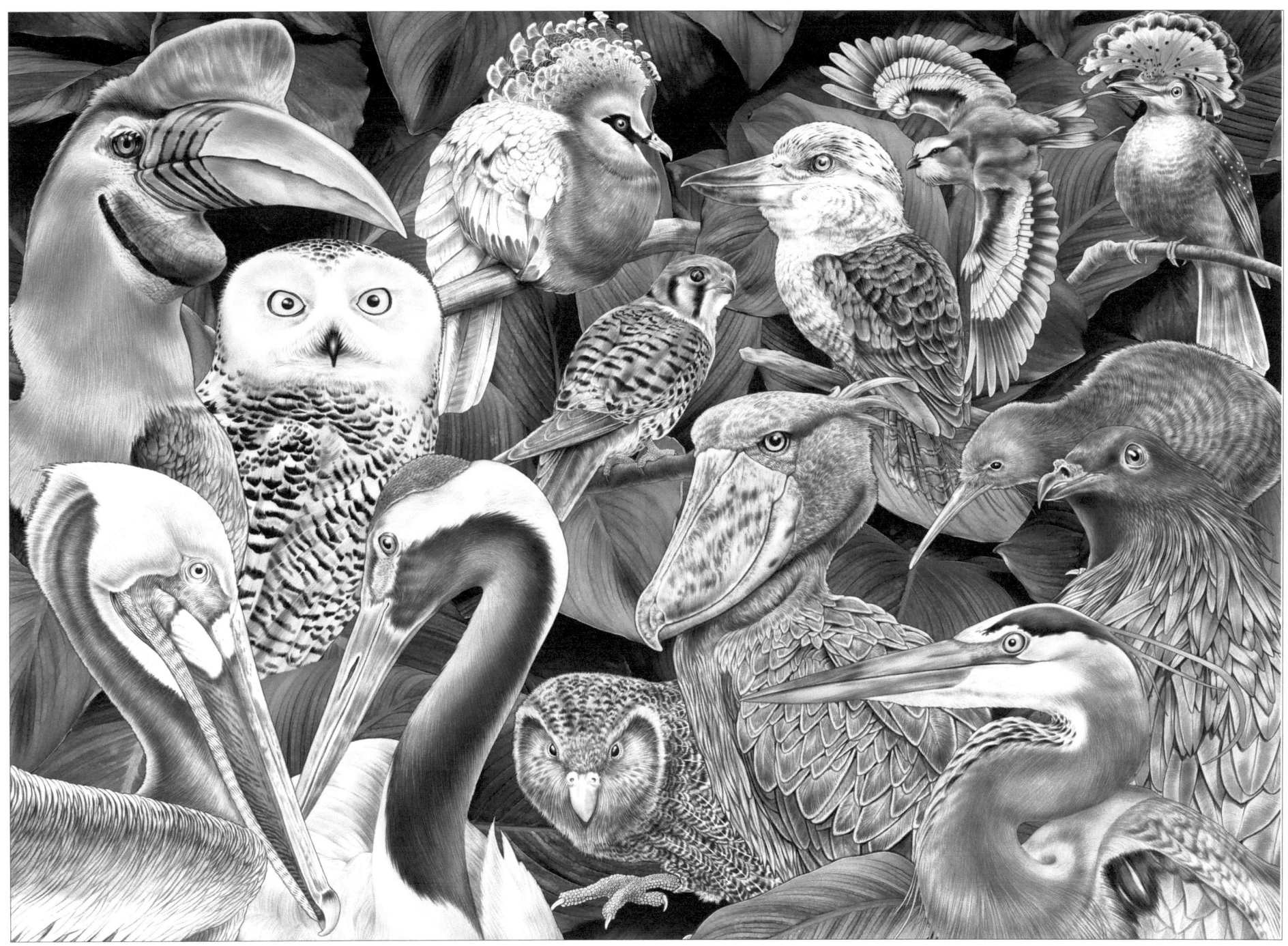
Birds of the World

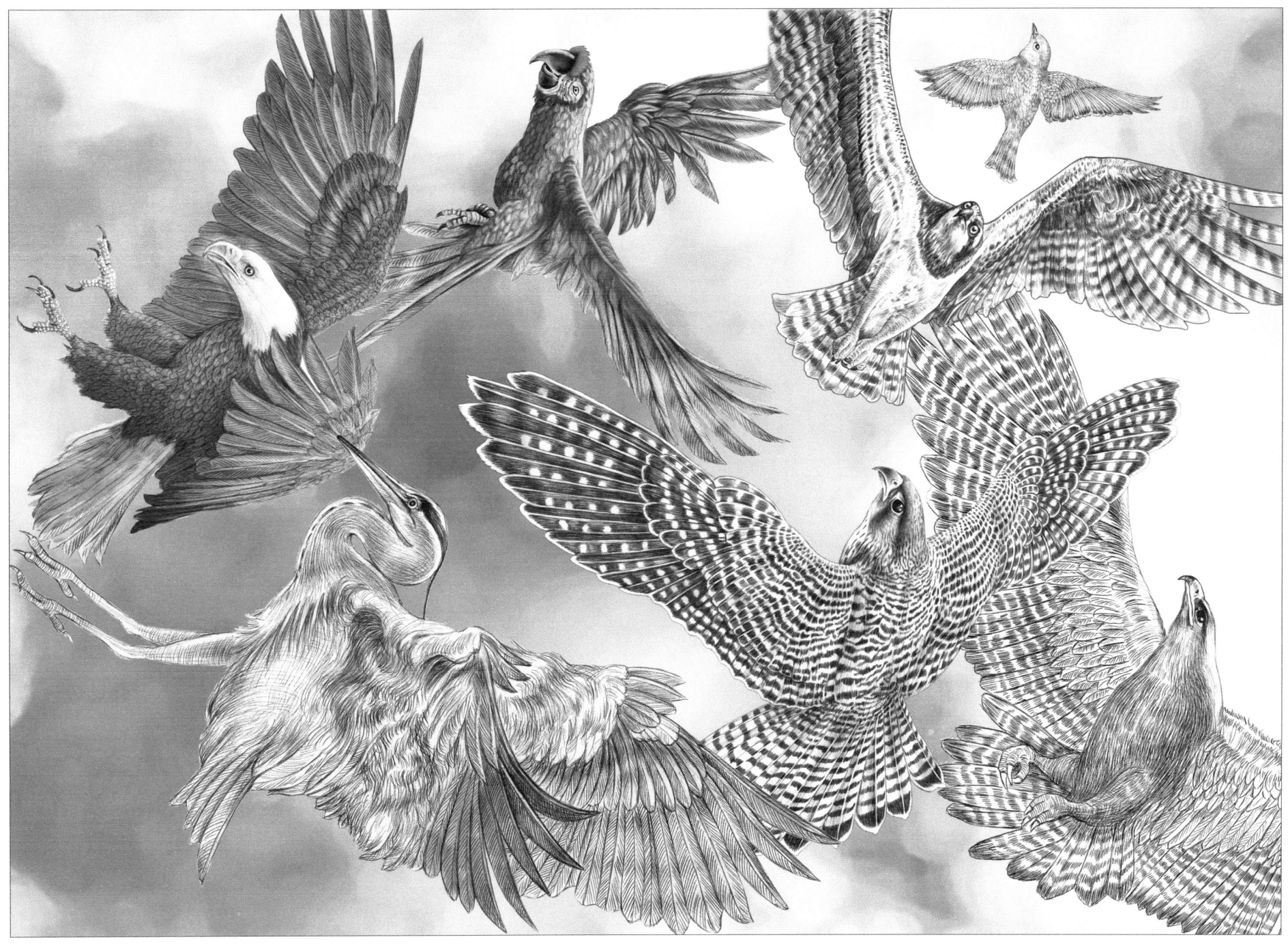
Birds in Flight

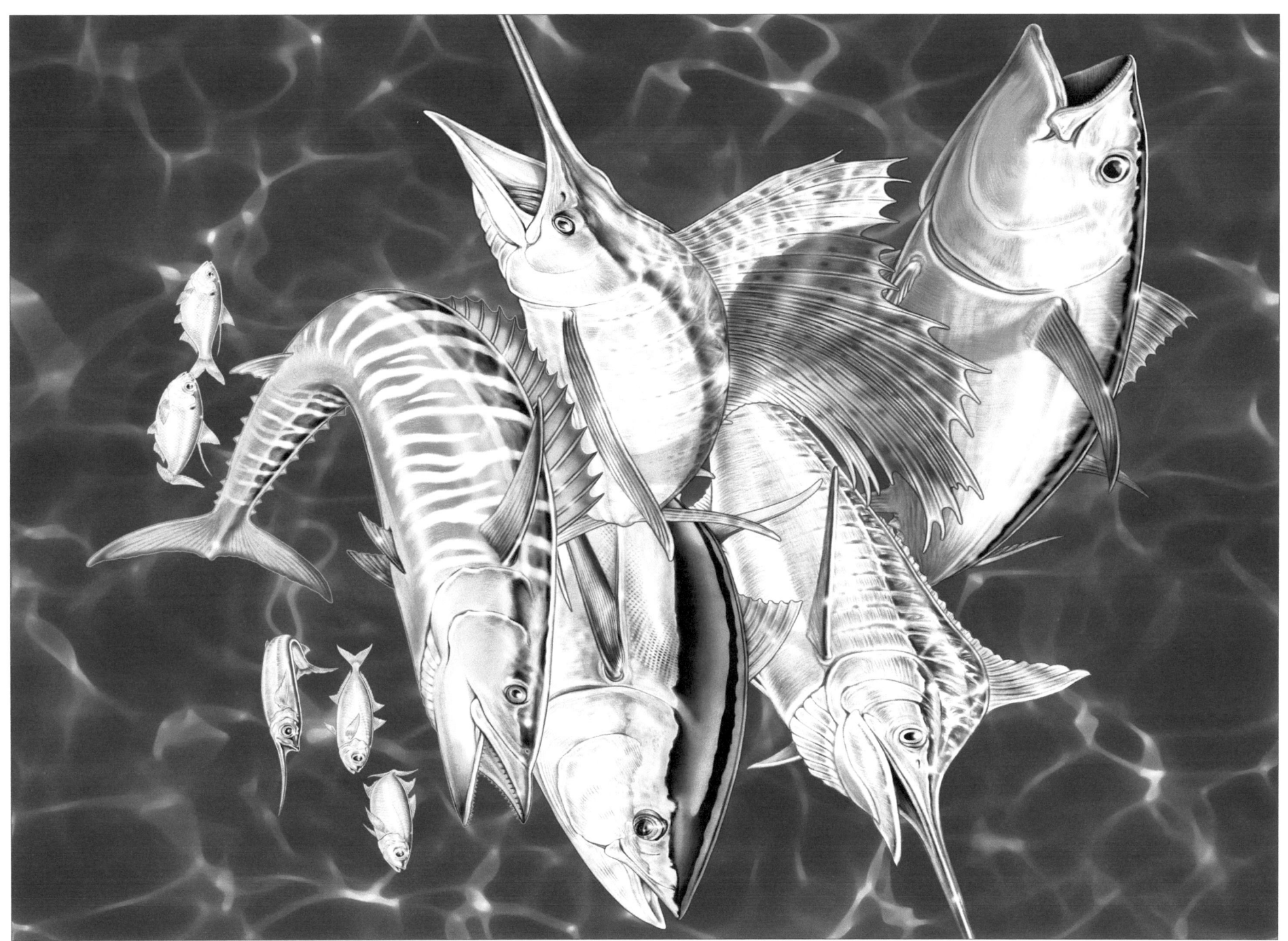
Deep Sea Fish

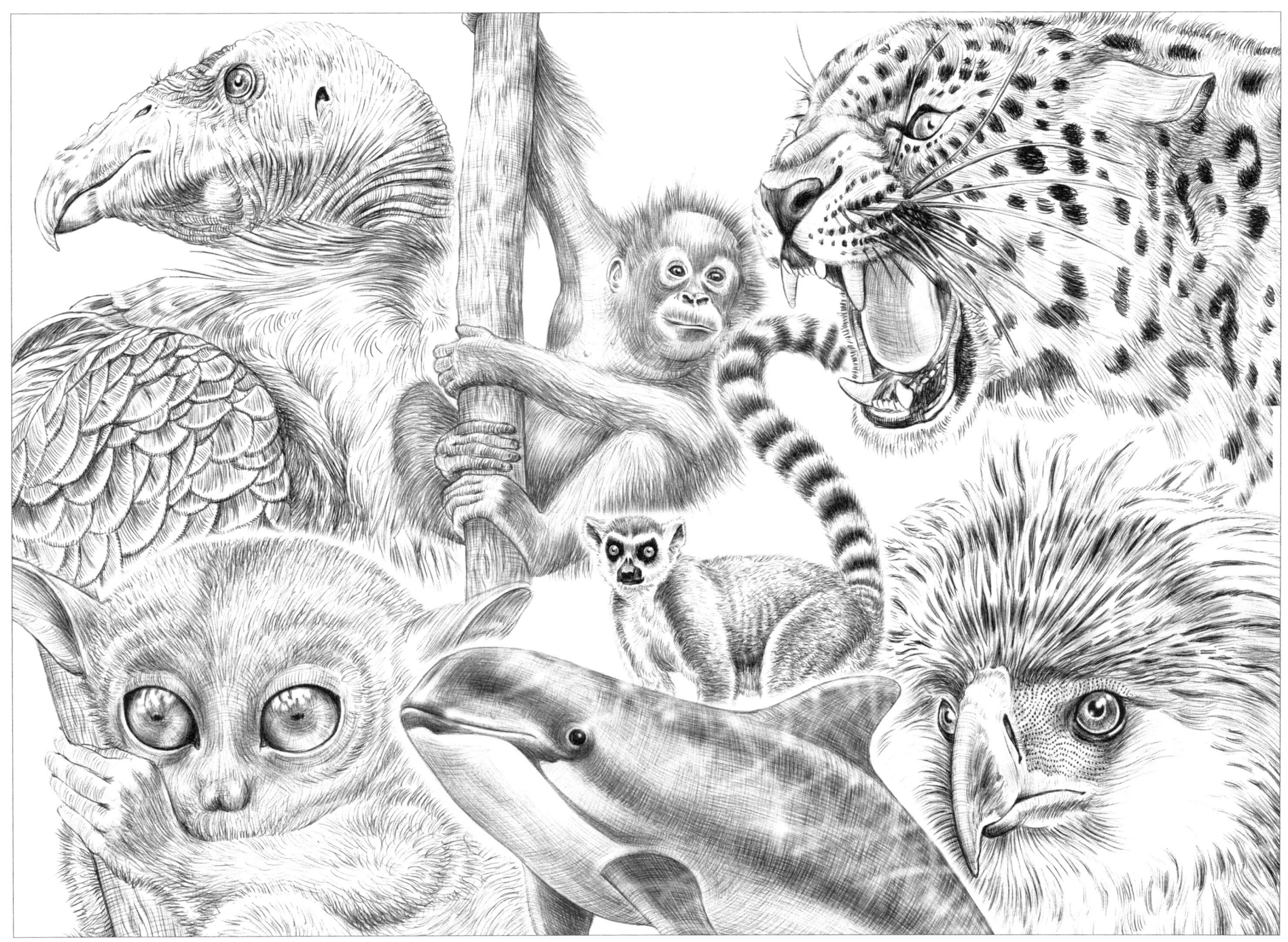

Endangered Species

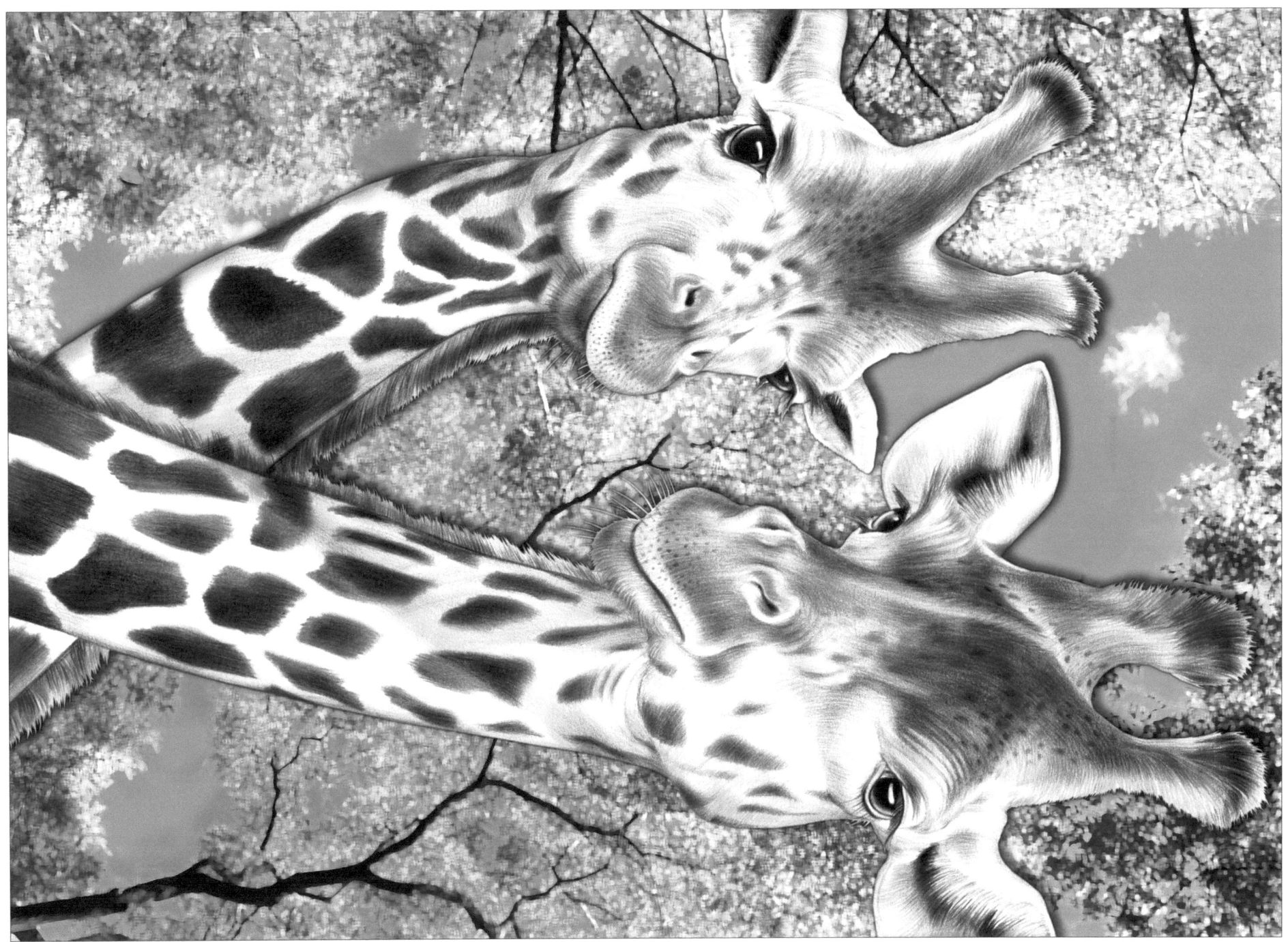

Giraffes

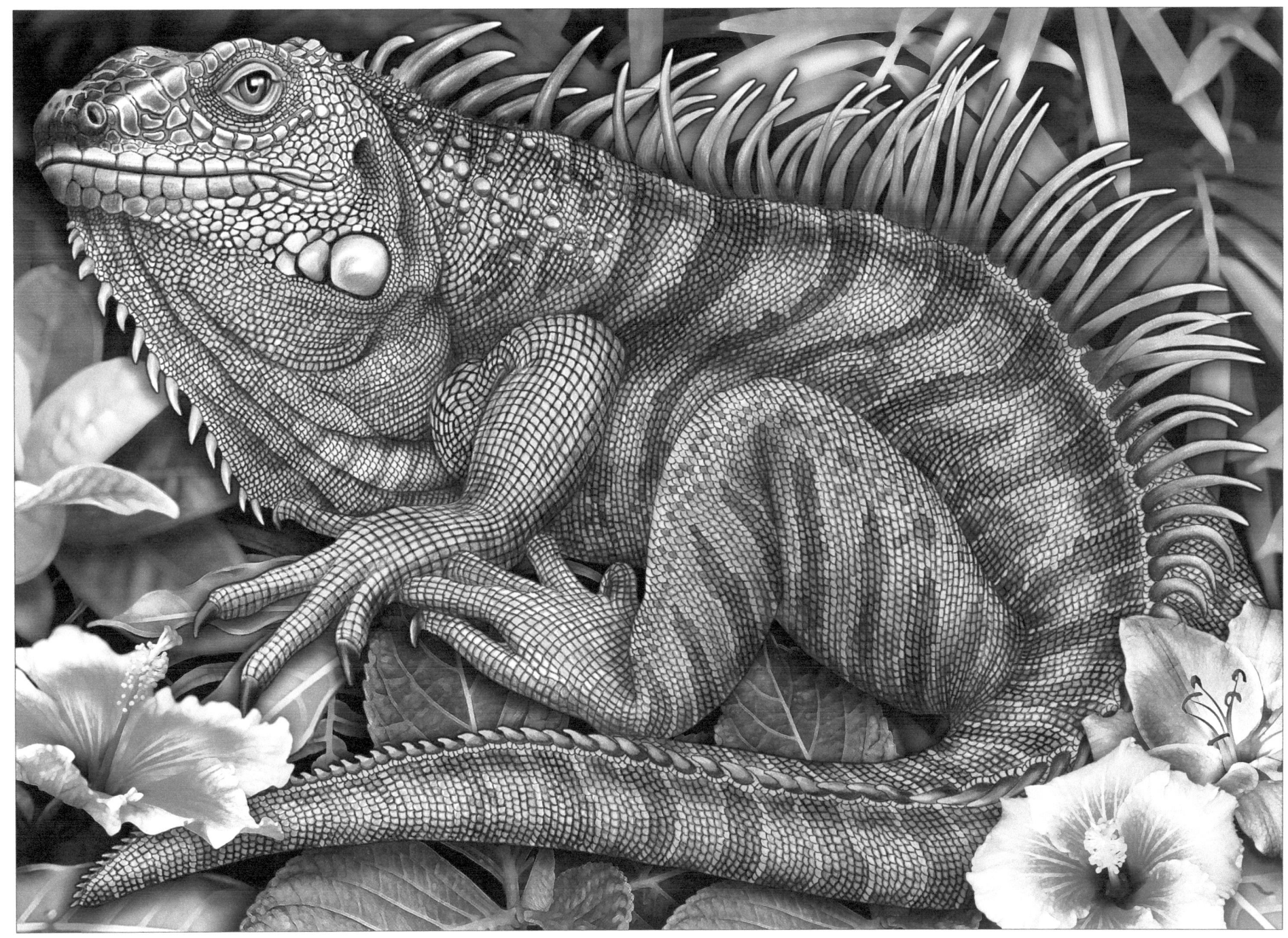

Iguana One

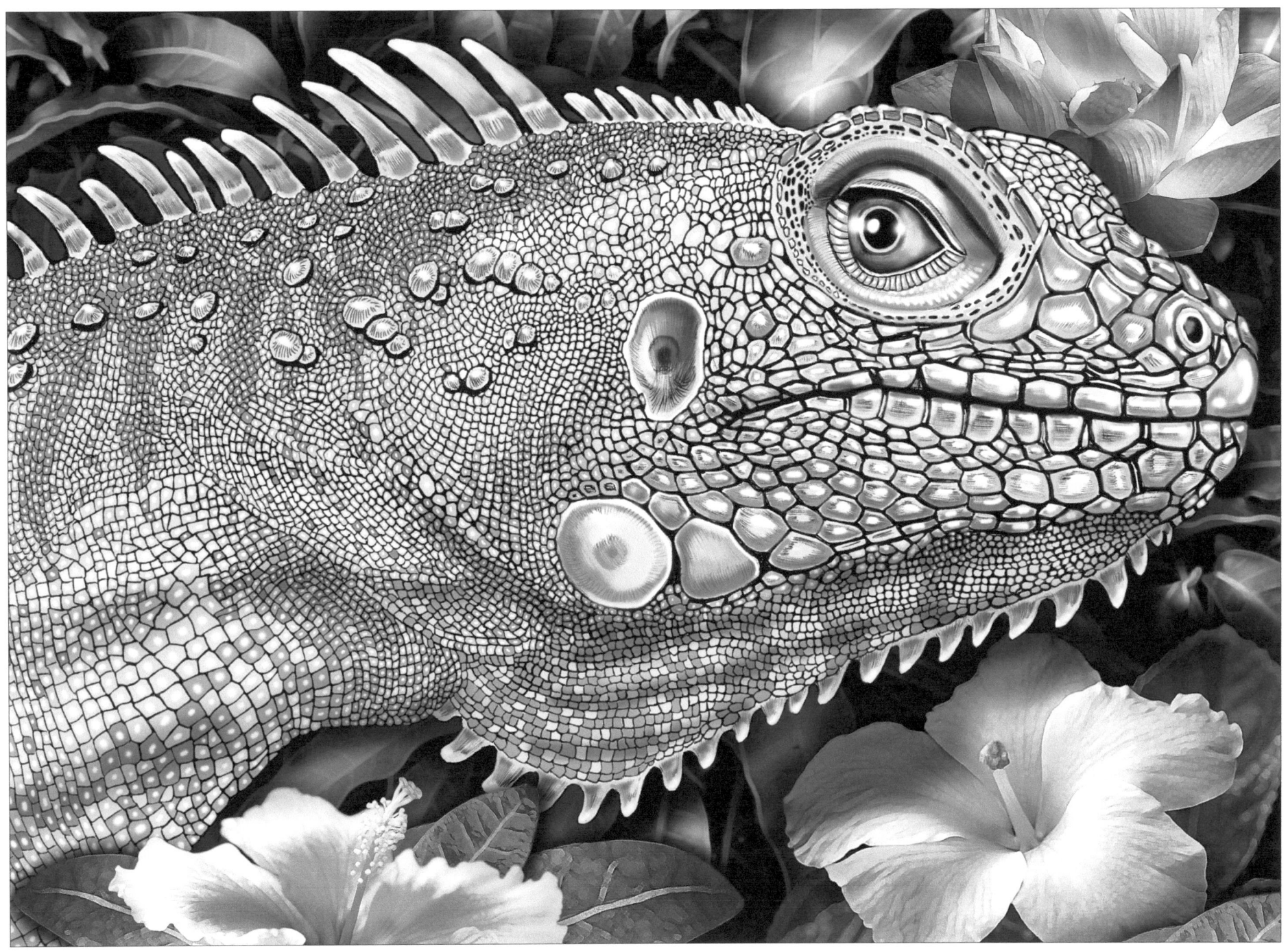

Iguana Two

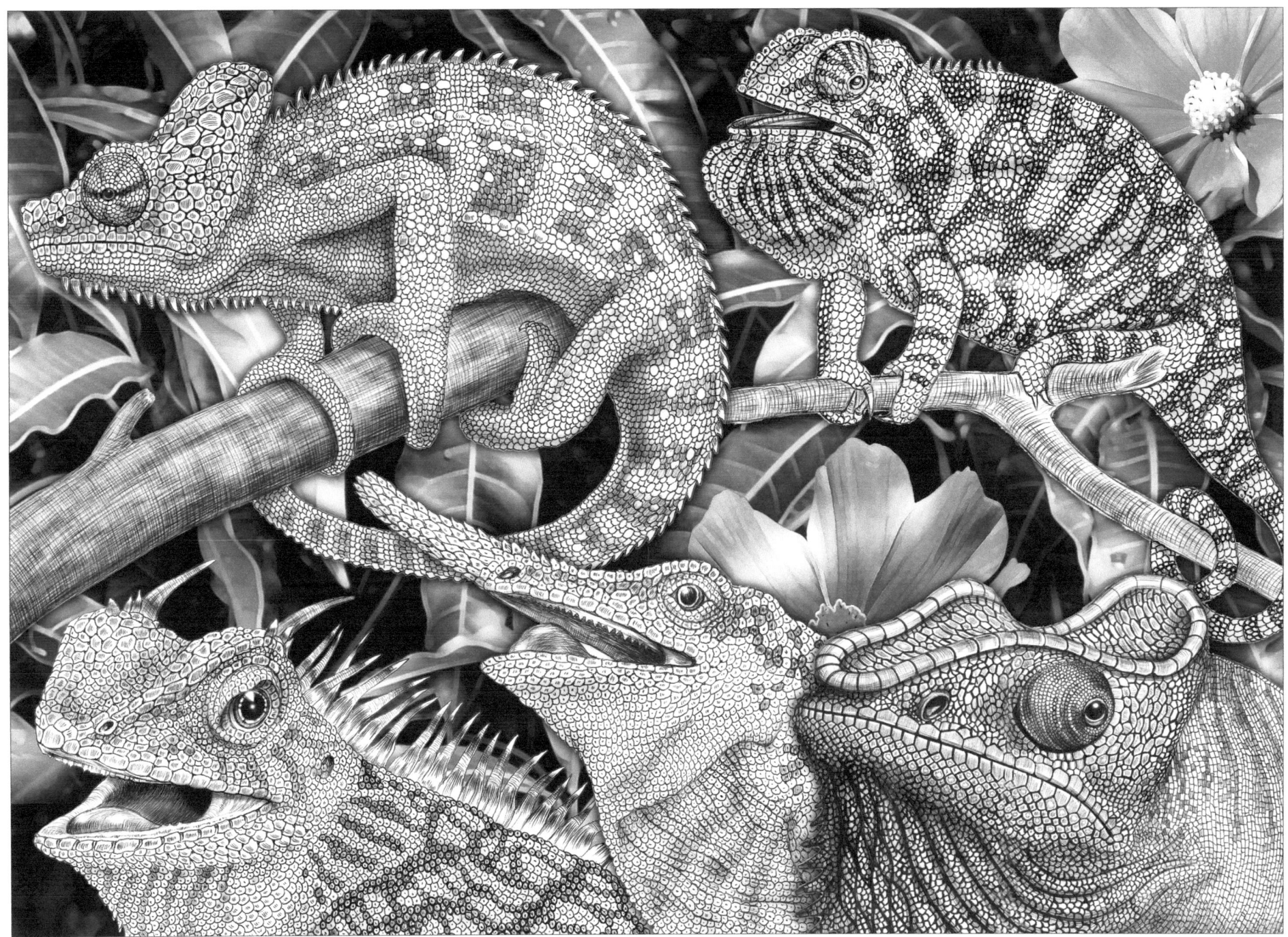

Lizards

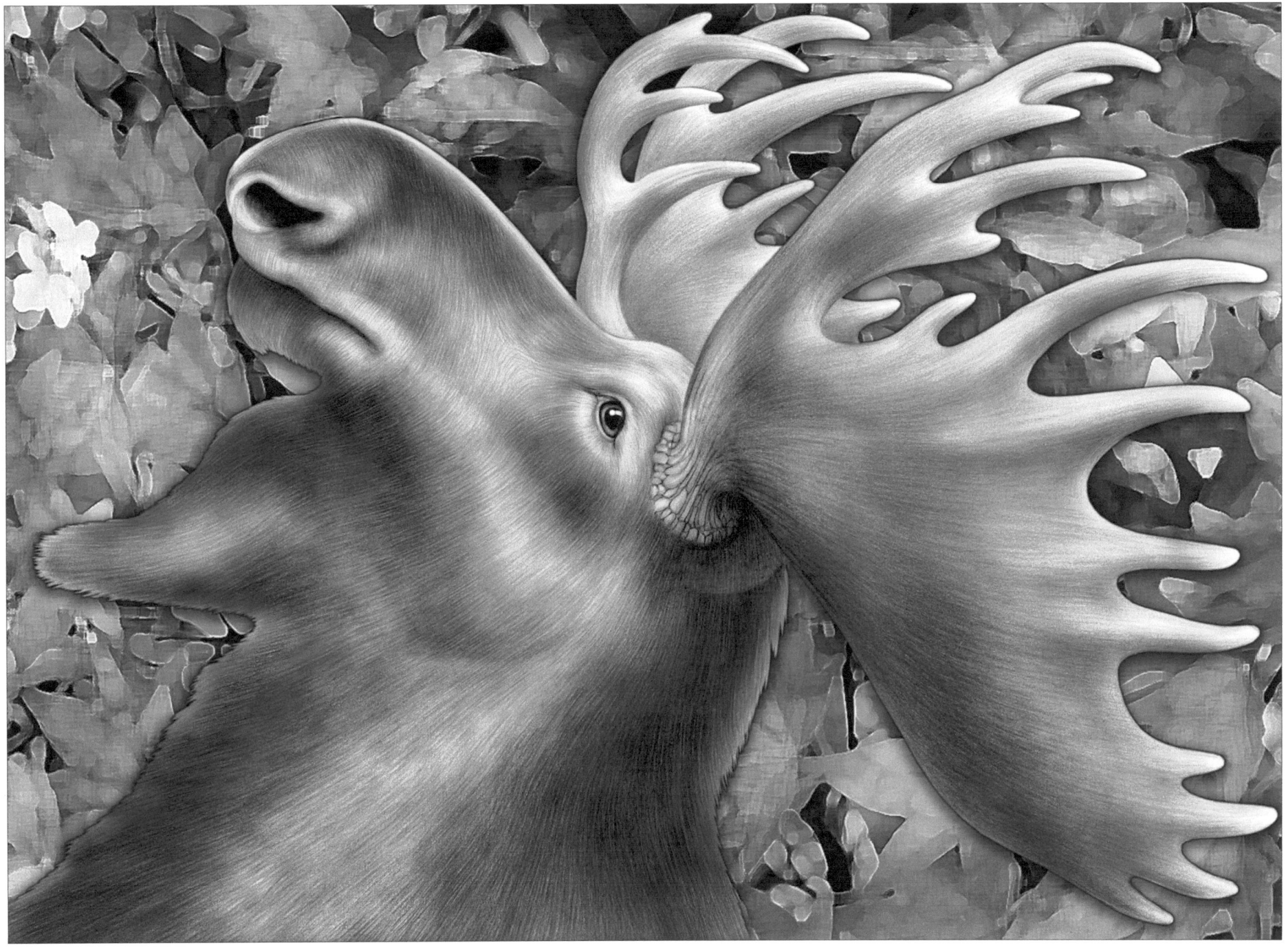

Moose

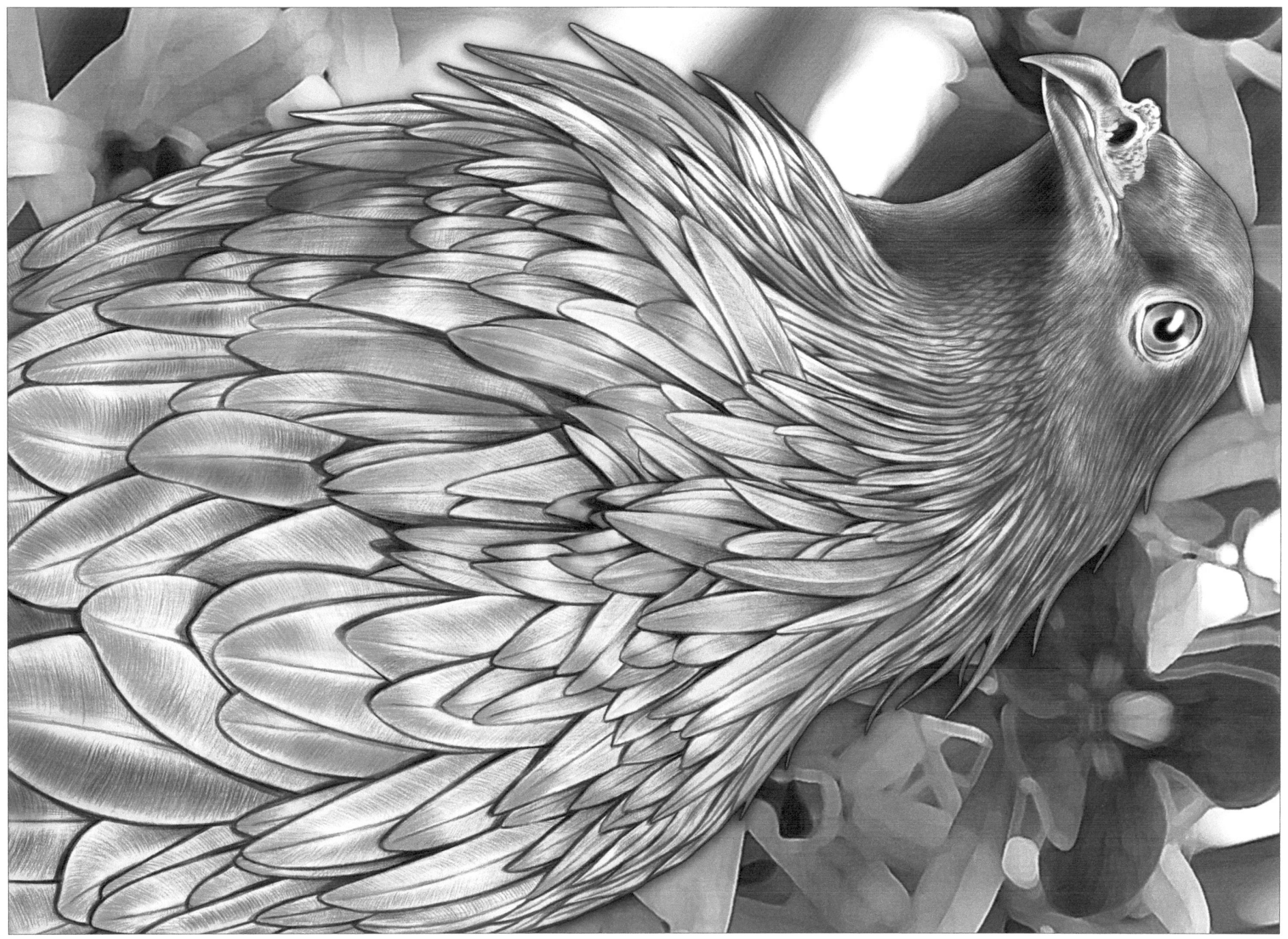

Nicobar Pigeon

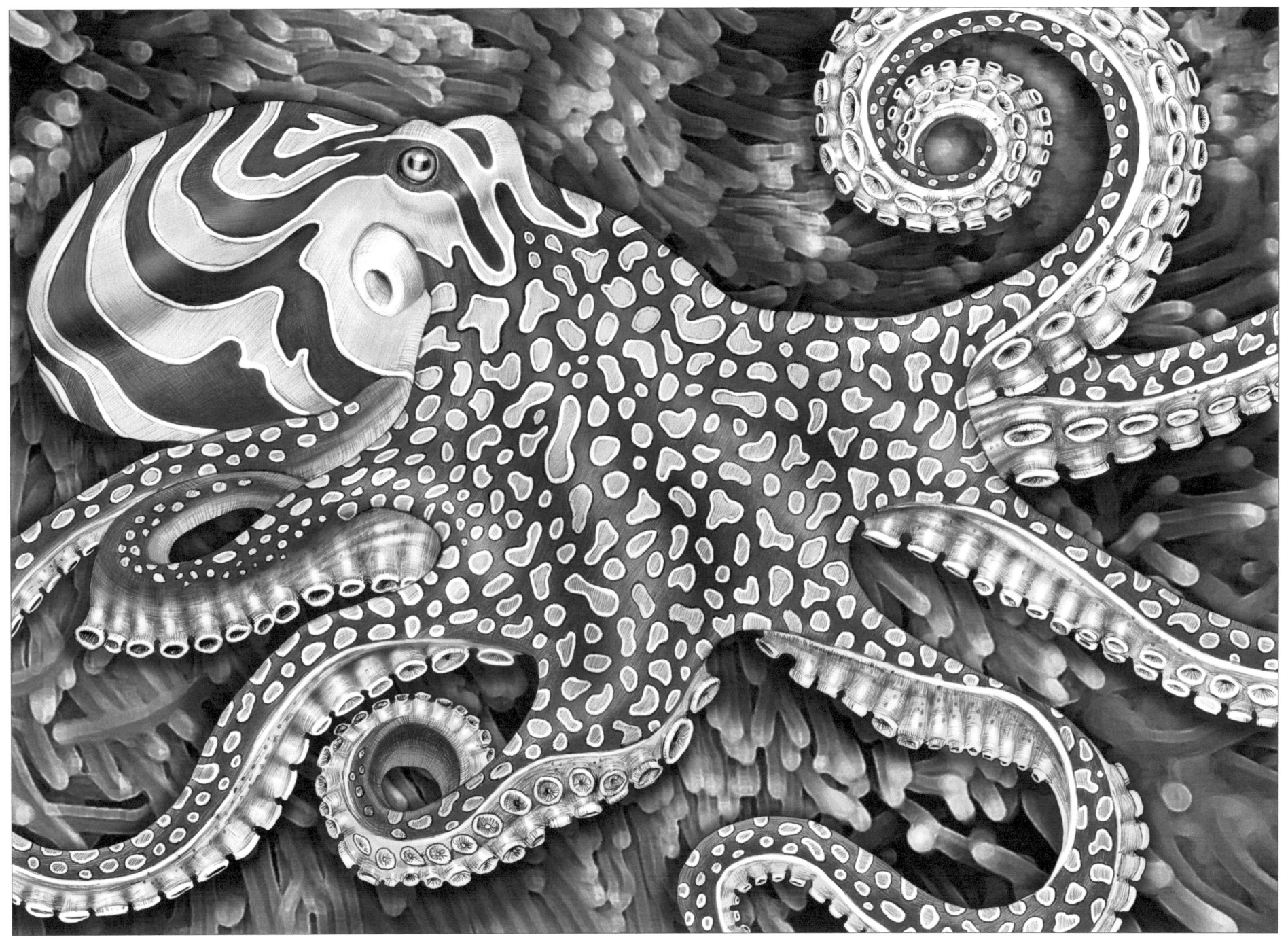

Octopus

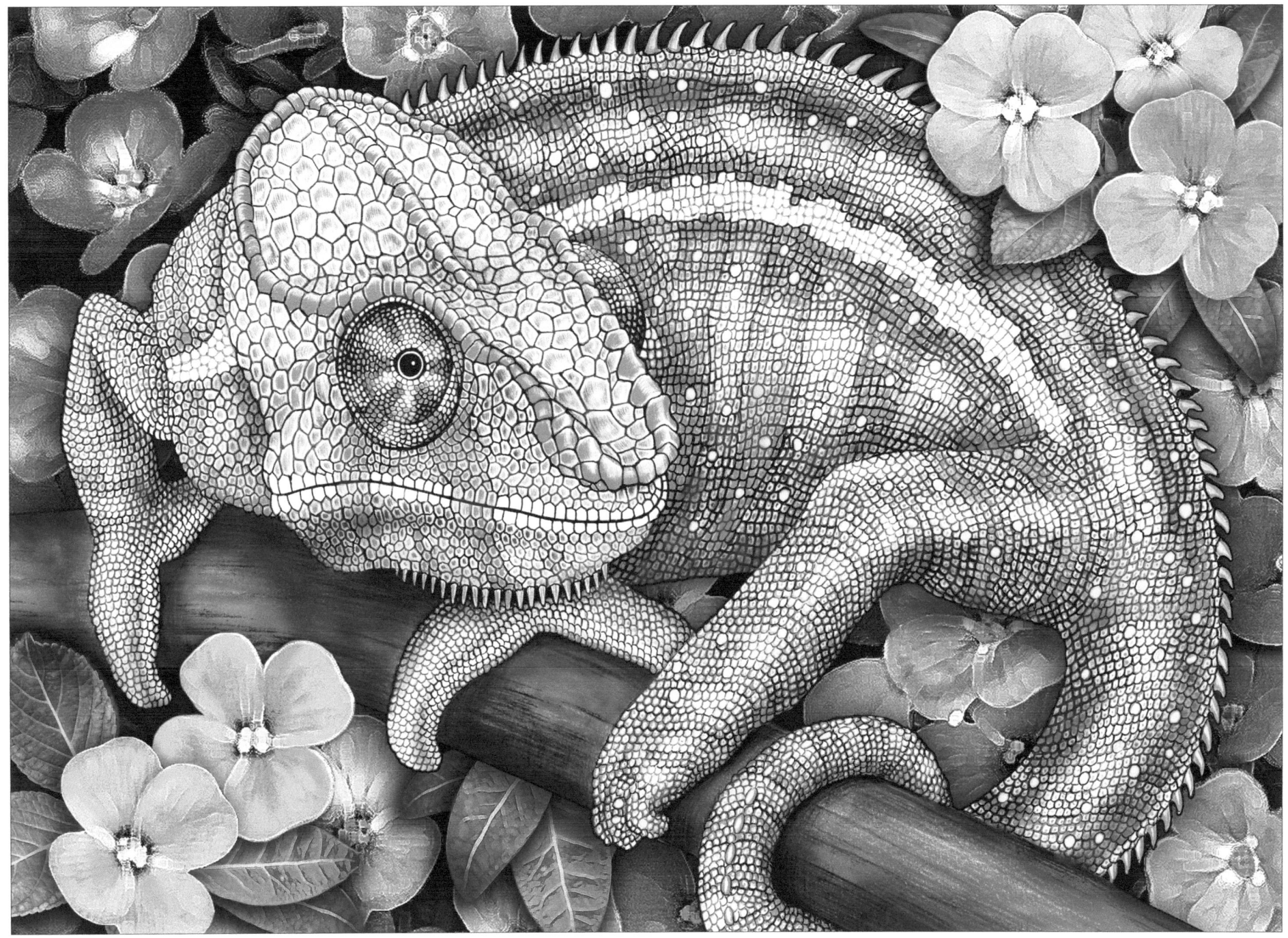

Panther Chameleon

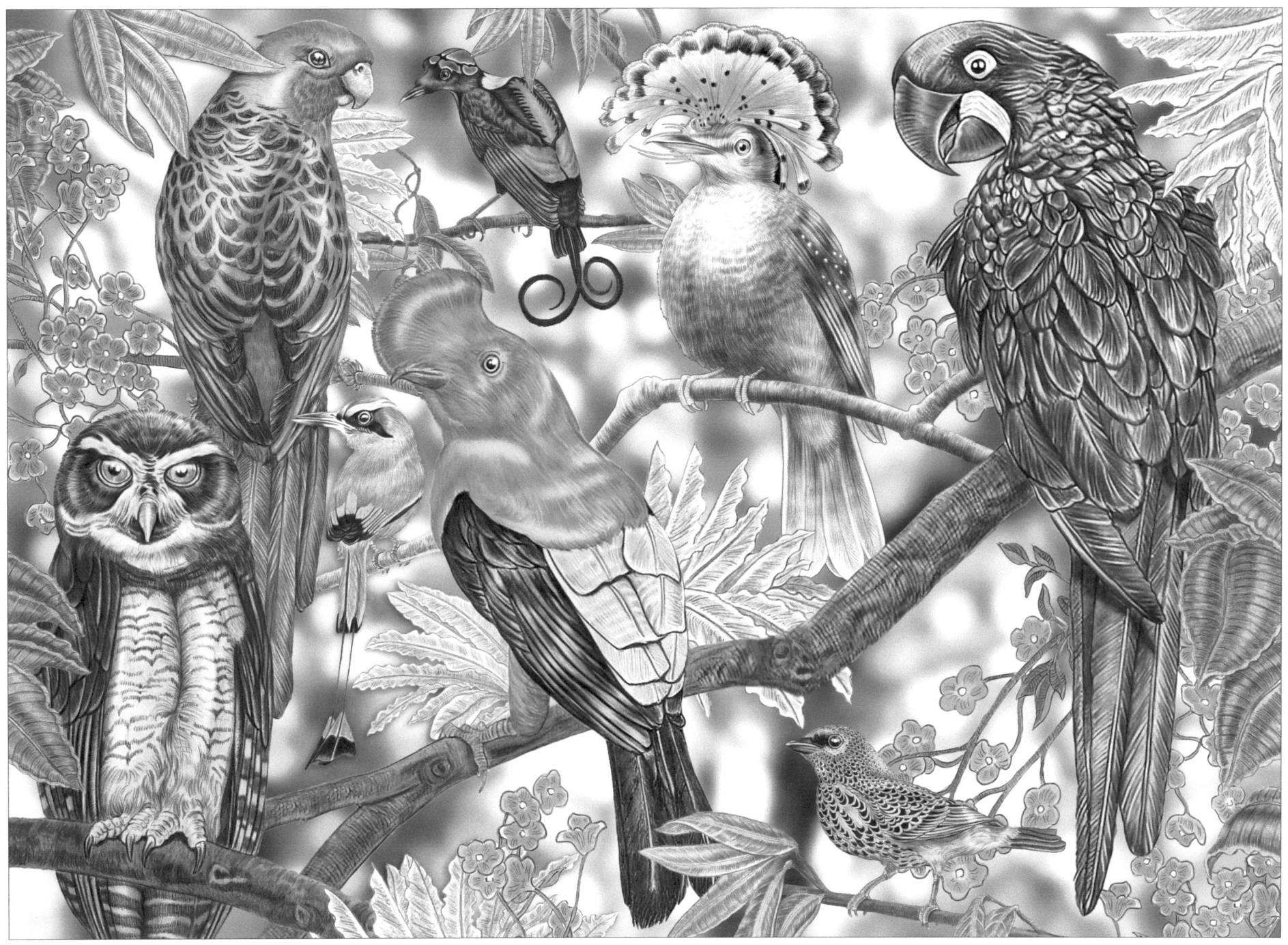

Rainforest Birds

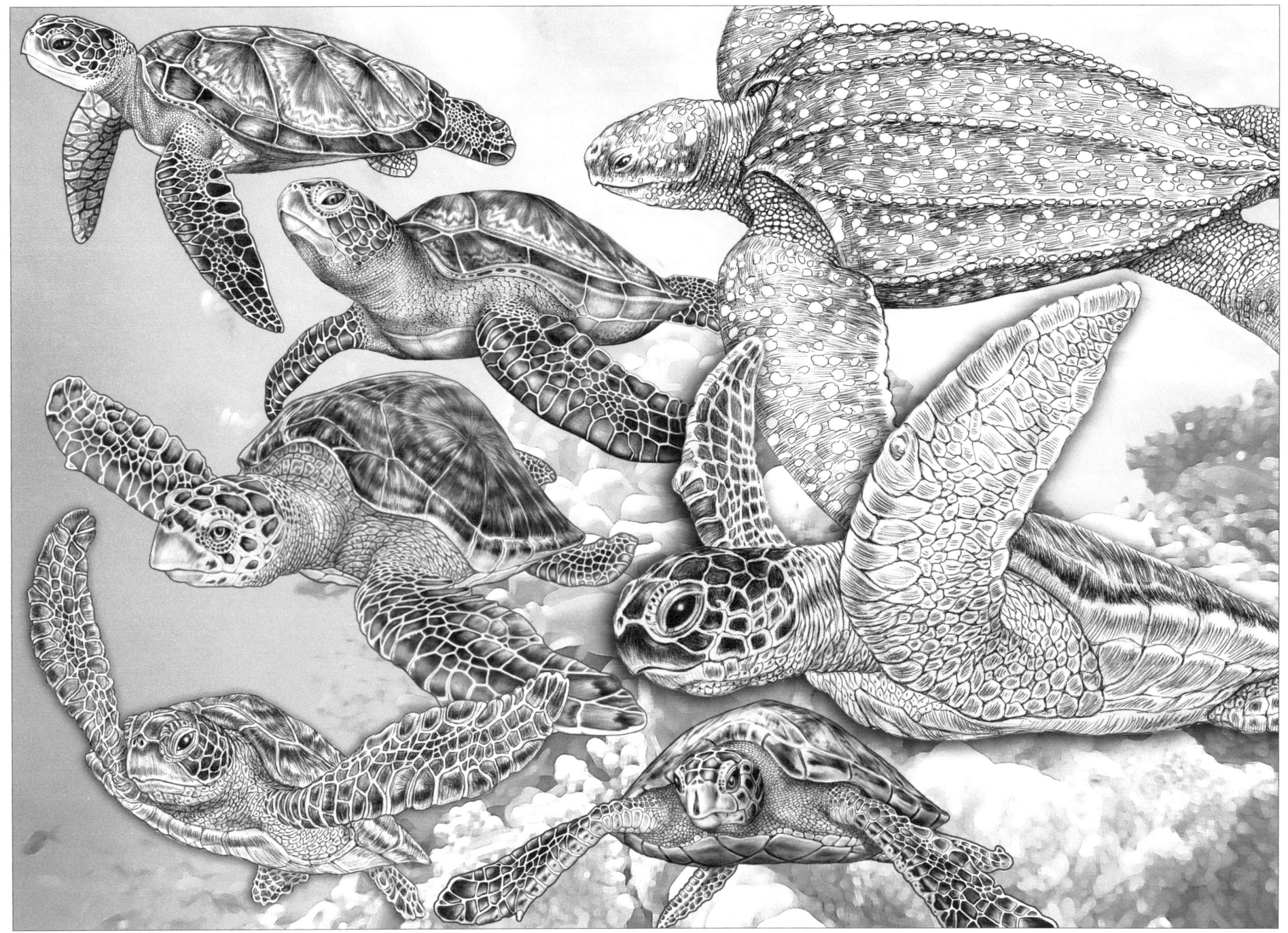
Sea Turtles

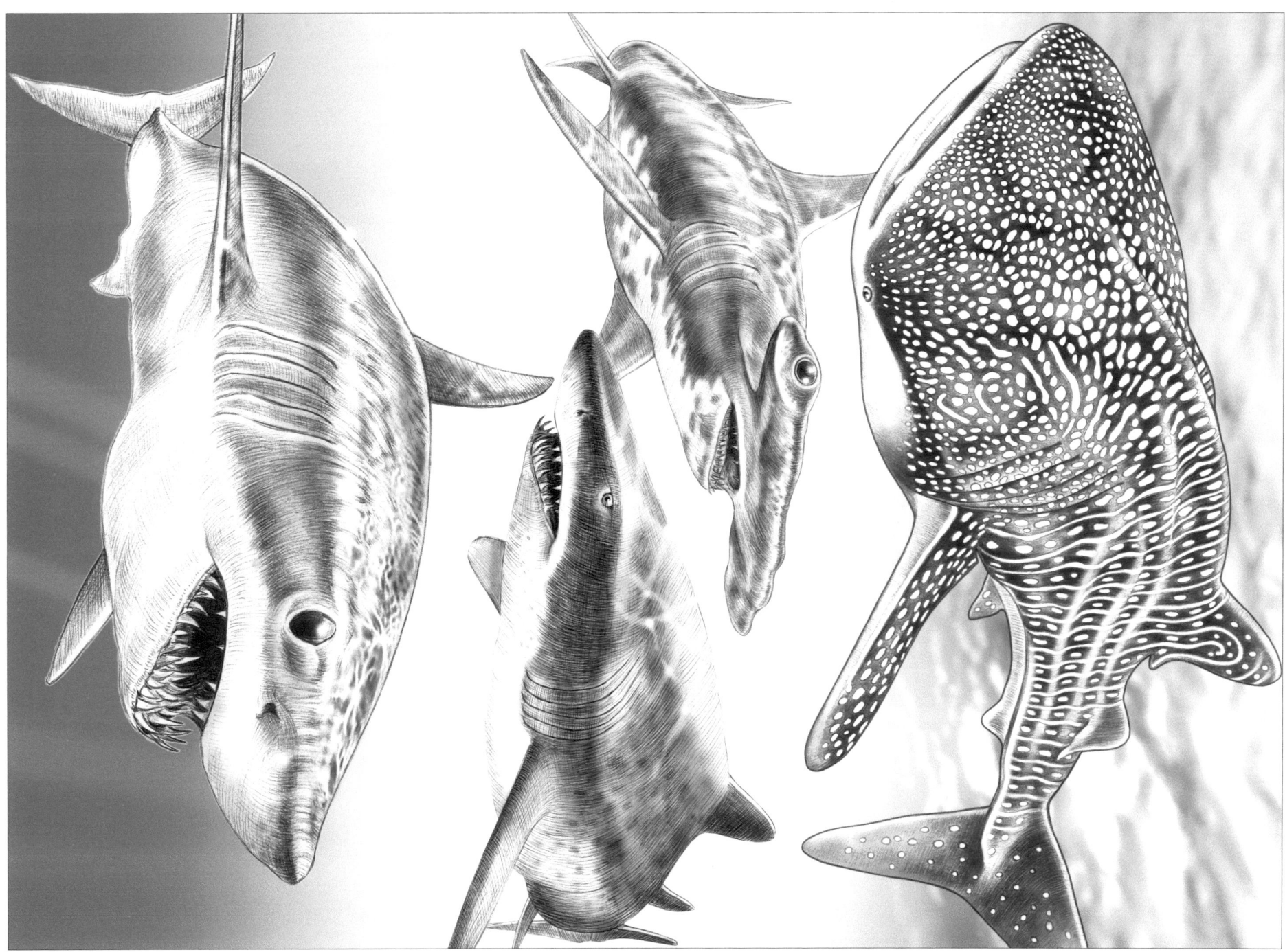

Sharks

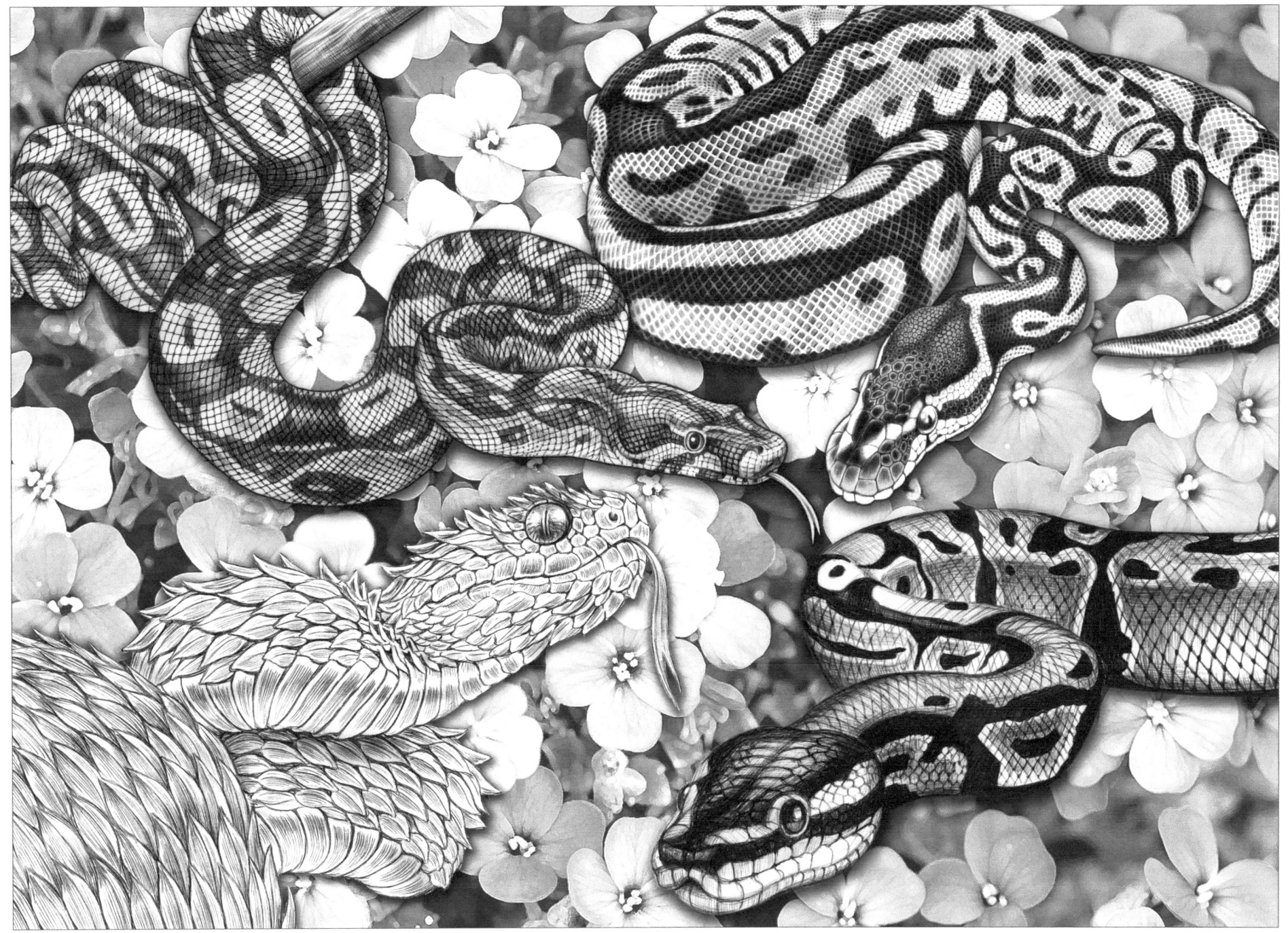
Snakes

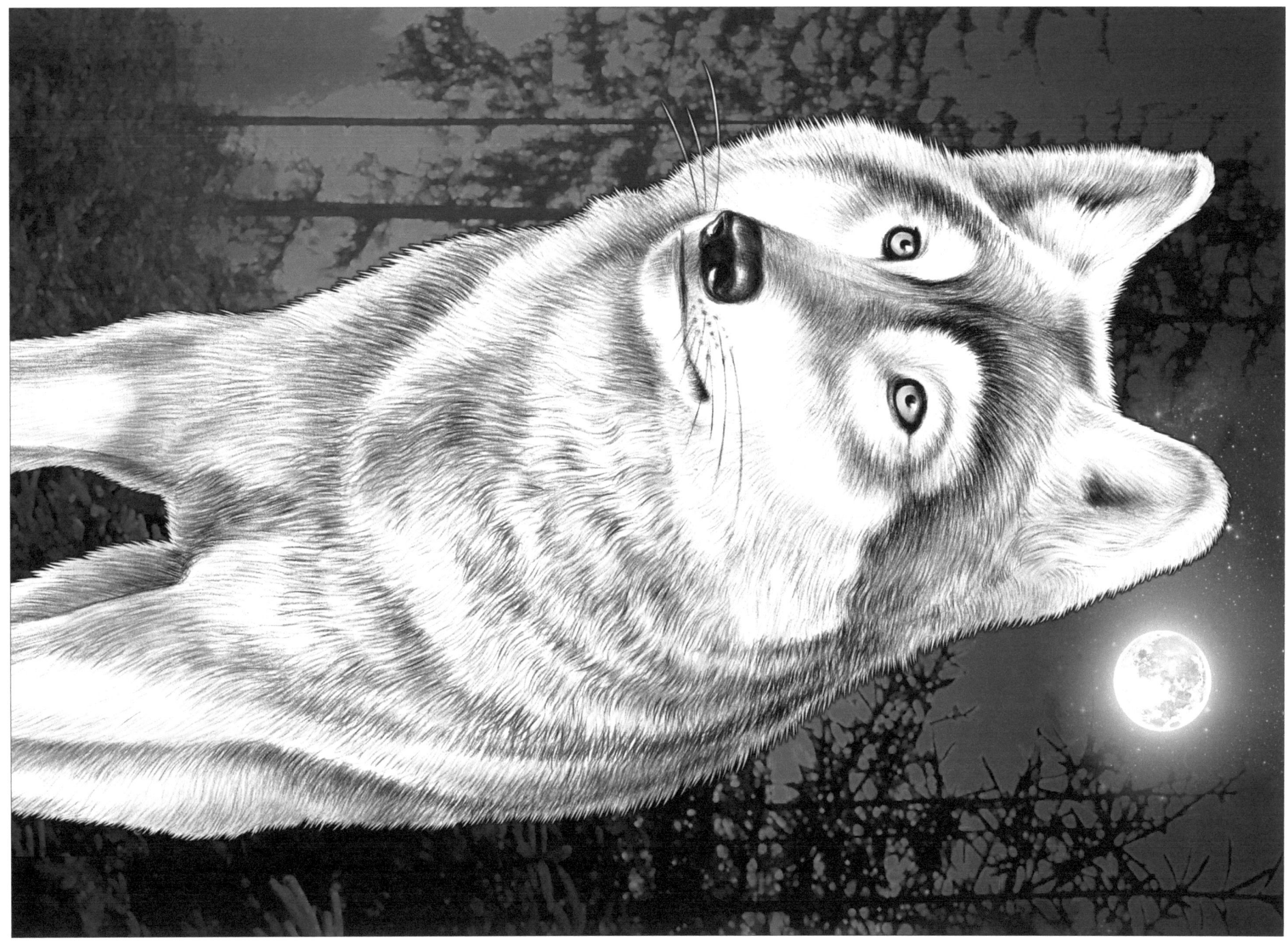

Timber Wolf

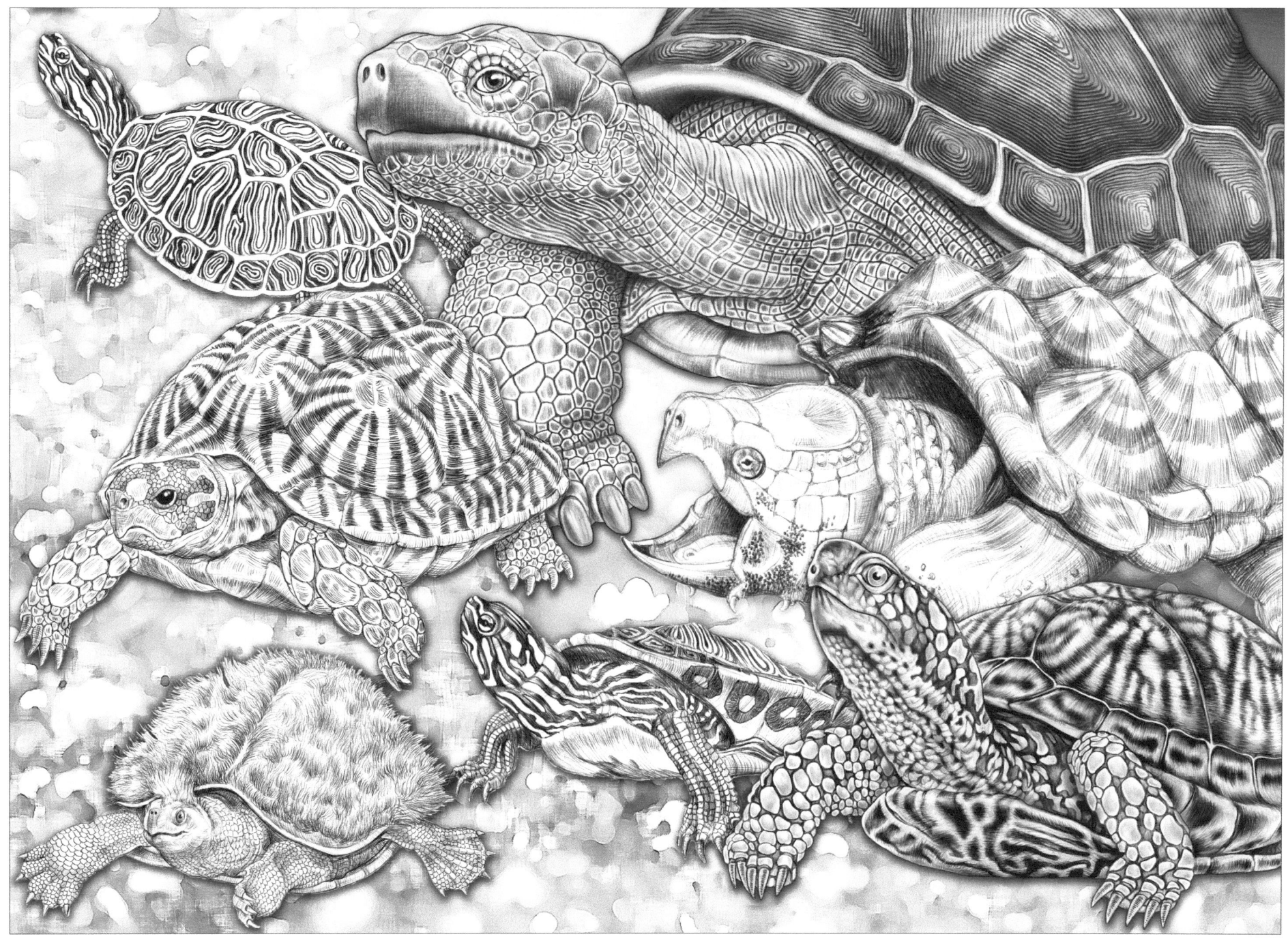
Turtles

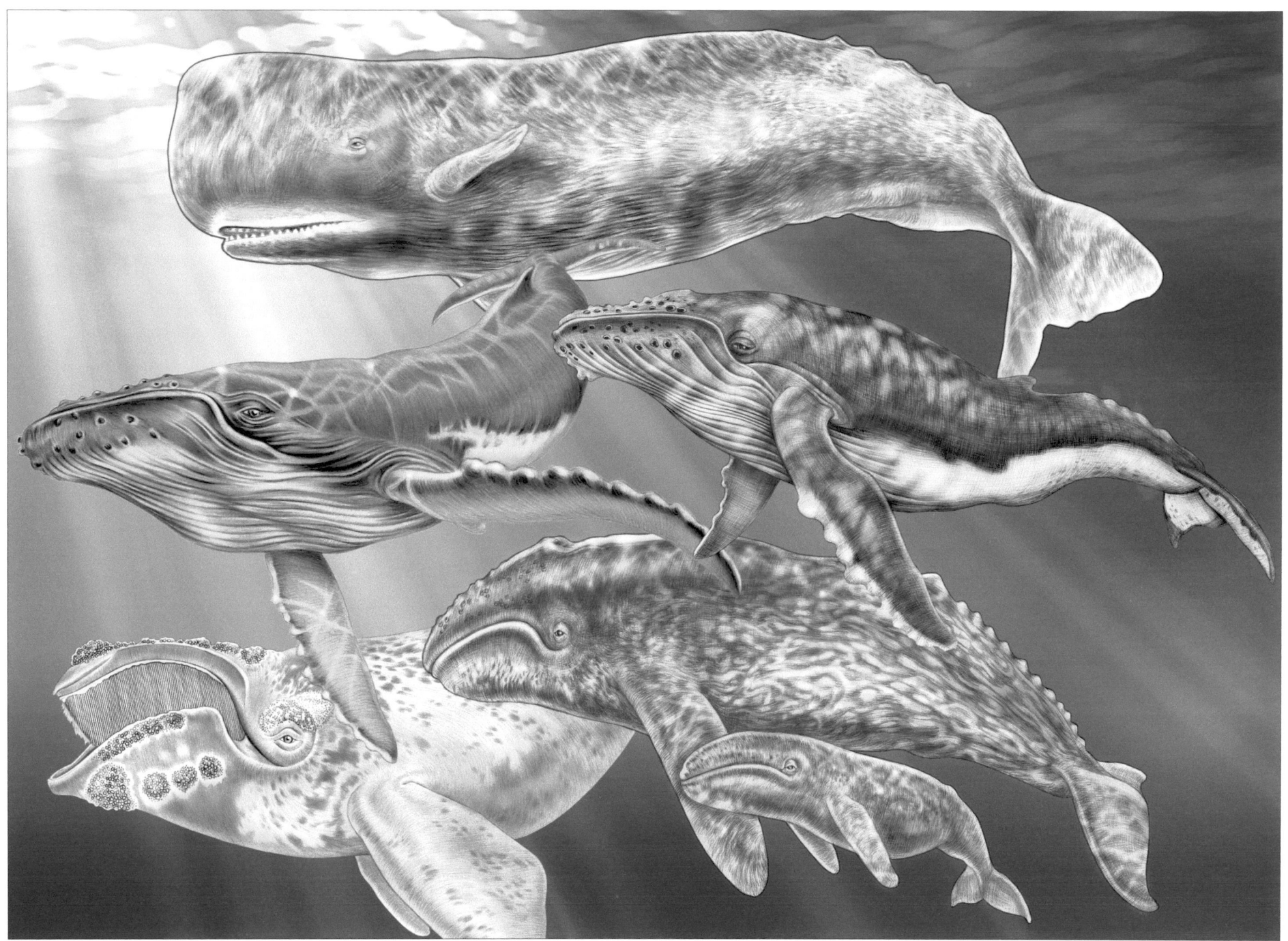
Whales

Tim Jeffs is a New York City based artist and illustrator who has been creating dynamic artwork for over 25 years. Animals are a favorite subject matter of his, along with the complex and intricate details these creatures possess. *"The incredible diversity and complexity of animals has always intrigued me. They offer endless pleasure to look and marvel upon. In every drawing I try to capture the unique quality of each particular animal. I hope you enjoy my perspective, love and admiration of these incredible creatures."*

Visit my website for prints, digital coloring books and coloring lessons:

www.TimJeffsArt.com

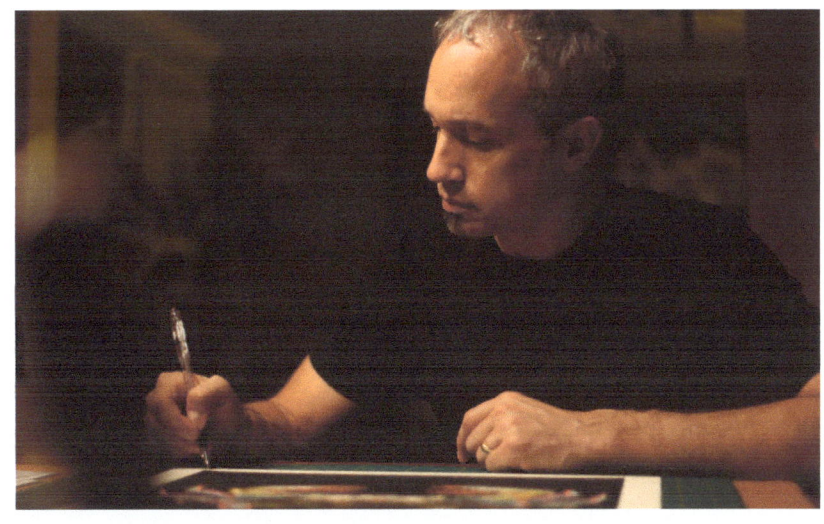

Discover the full line of Tim Jeffs' Published Coloring Books

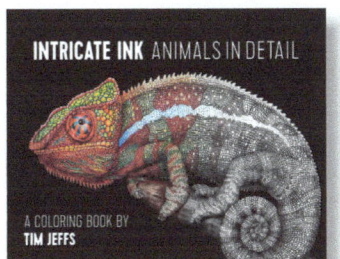 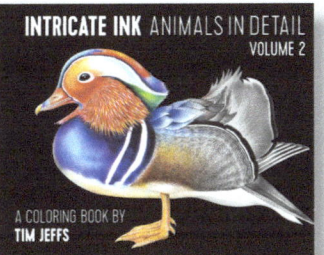 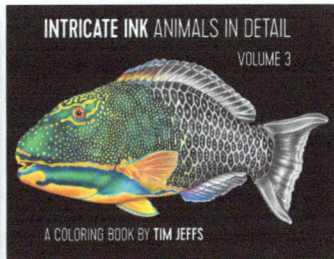 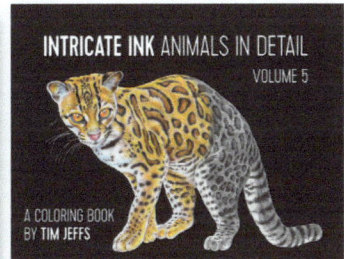 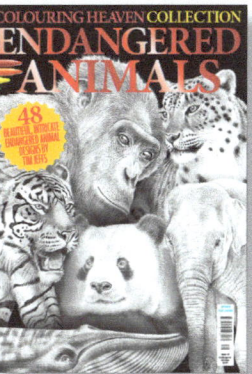

Intricate Ink Animals In Detail Volume 1, 2 3 and 5, and Intricate Animal Drawings Volume 1 and 2 are available at:
Amazon.com
Bookdepository.com

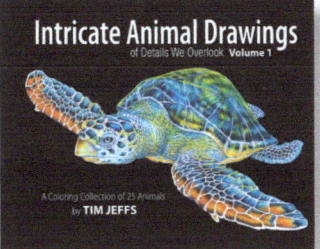 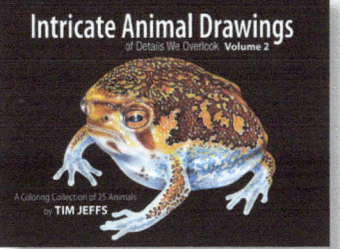

Colouring Heaven Collection Endangered Animals
Available at: Colouringheaven.com

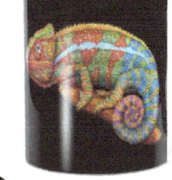

Discover Tim Jeffs' Merchandise

Etsy Shop
www.etsy.com/shop/TimJeffsArt

Society6 Shop
www.society6.com/TimJeffsArt

Redbubble Shop
TimJeffsArt.redbubble.com

TeePublic Shop
https://www.teepublic.com/user/tim-jeffs-art

Discover the full line of Tim Jeffs Coloring Books and Lessons at:

TimJeffsArt.com
Etsy.com • Amazon.com

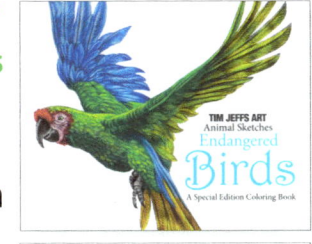 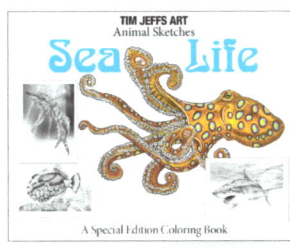 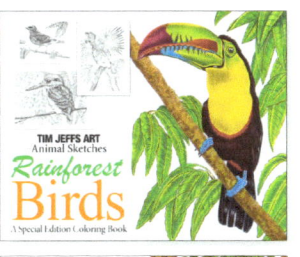 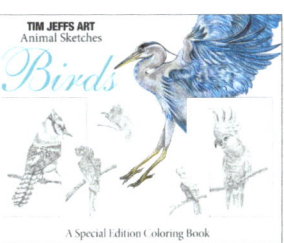 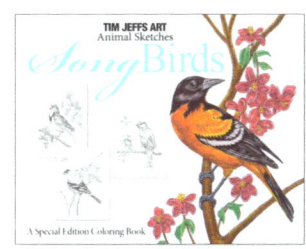
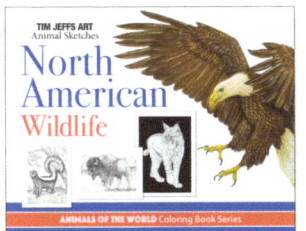 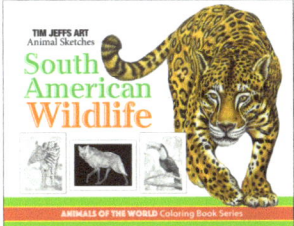 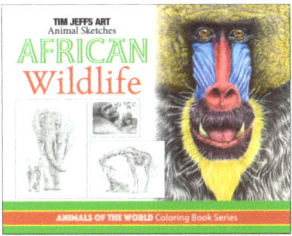 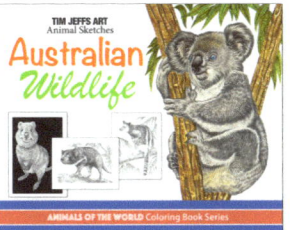 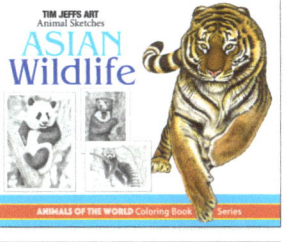 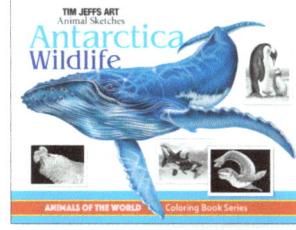
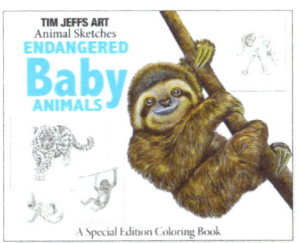 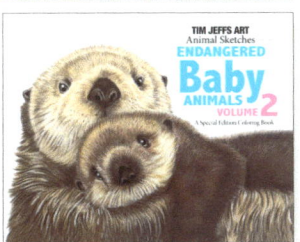 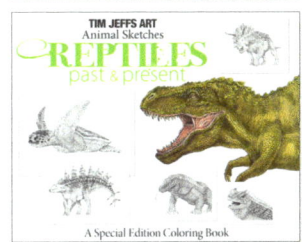 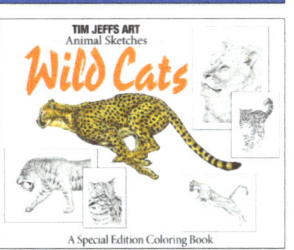 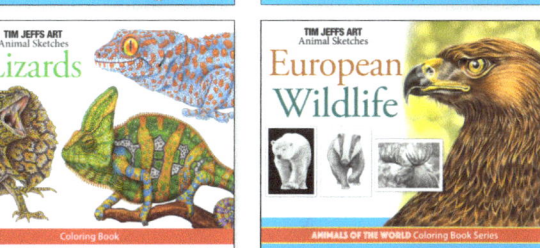
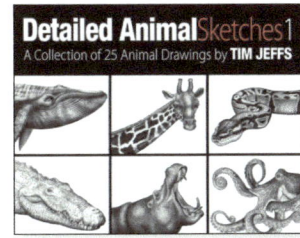 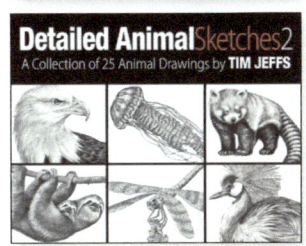 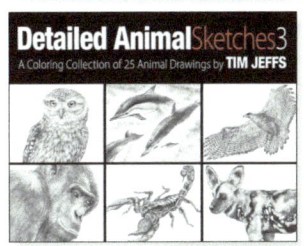 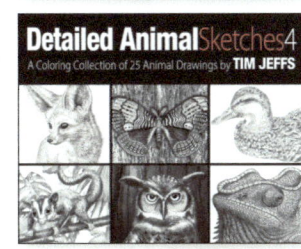 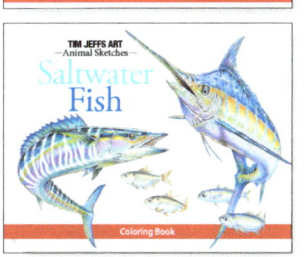 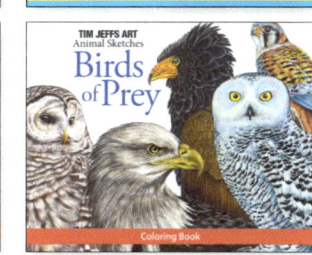
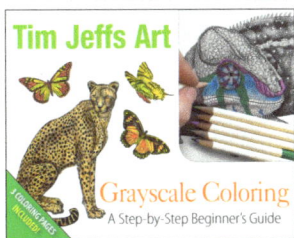 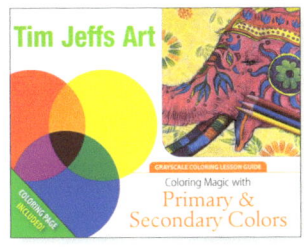 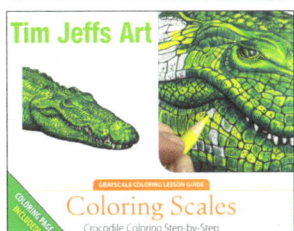 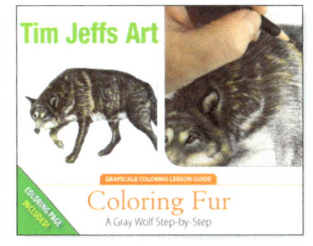 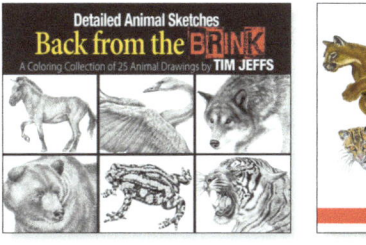 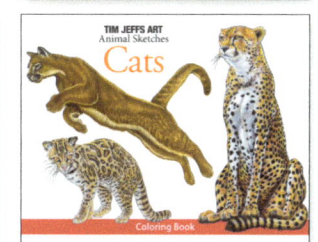
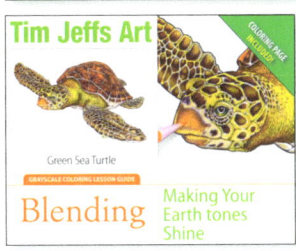 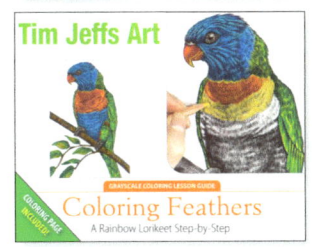 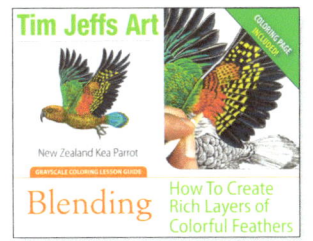 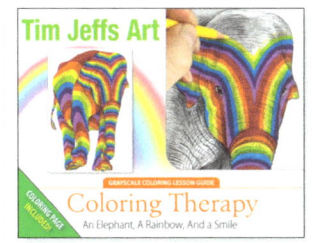 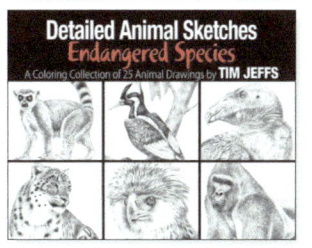 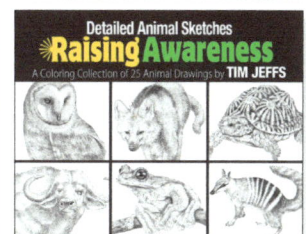

TIM JEFFS ART Online Resources

Share Your Creativity with the World!

Join the ever-expanding coloring group of animal lovers who inspire each other through their colorings of the animals from Tim's books and lessons. With thousands of members from all around the world, Tim's Facebook group "Intricate Ink Coloring Group" is a creative and safe space where everyone is welcome. Jo Warren, the groups all-inspiring administrator will welcome you in with open arms and is there to encourage everyone to just have fun no matter your coloring skill level. Come join, we can't wait to have you as a member! Join Tim's Facebook Coloring Group at:

www.facebook.com/groups/intricateink

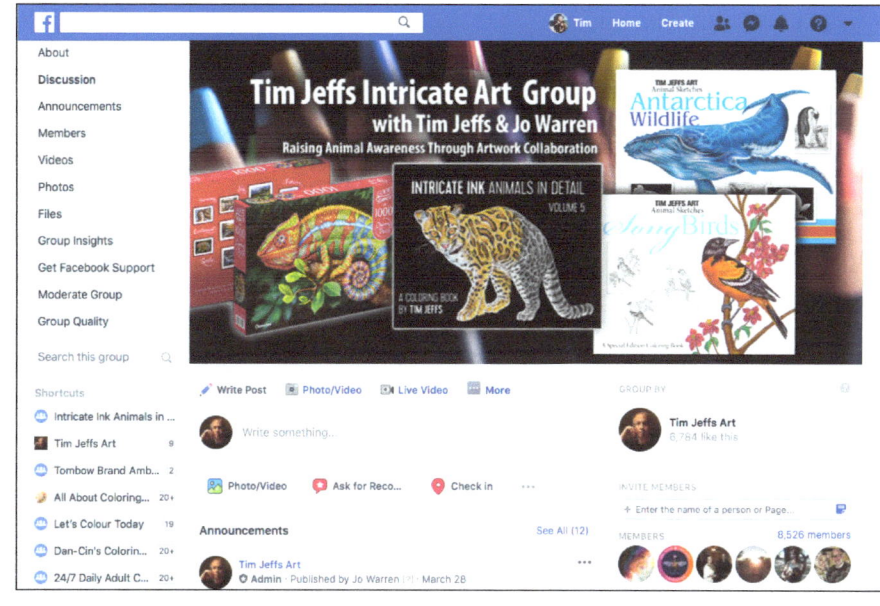

Visit the Home of Tim Jeffs Art

TimJeffsArt.com is my home on the web where I display all of my work and various projects. I hope you can stop by for a visit! You'll find my new shop where signed and unsigned prints of all of my animal drawings are available to purchase, along with the complete library of my digital download coloring books and grayscale coloring lessons. In the conservation section, you can see the projects that I am very proud of. Using my art to preserve wildlife is so important to me.

www.TimJeffsArt.com

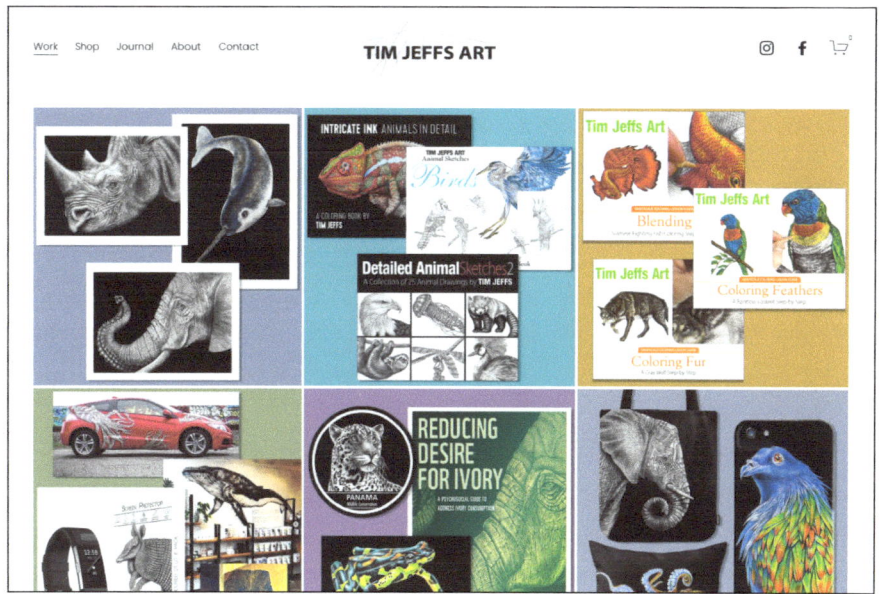